First Fabulous Facts

My Body

Written by Jaclyn Crupi

Illustrated by Patrizia Donaera

Cartoon illustrations by Jane Porter

Consultant: Dr Kim Dennis-Bryan

Educational consultant: Geraldine Taylor

A catalogue record for this book is available from the British Library

Published by Ladybird Books Ltd
80 Strand, London, WC2R 0RL
A Penguin Company

001
© LADYBIRD BOOKS LTD MMXIV
LADYBIRD and the device of a Ladybird are trademarks of Ladybird Books Ltd

ISBN: 978-0-71819-355-3

Printed in China

Contents

My amazing body!

Unless you are an identical twin, nobody else in the whole world looks like you. People are different shapes and sizes and we all have different coloured hair, eyes and skin. Your body can do lots of amazing things because all of its different parts work together.

Fabulous Facts

Skin and bones

An adult has about 200 bones in their body. These make up the human skeleton. Muscles are attached to the skeleton and everything is covered in skin.

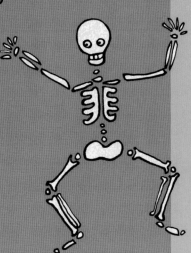

We are family

The way you look depends on your mum and dad and other relatives in your family. Who do you look like?

You have my eyes!

I love my family!

Wow!

Every single person has their own set of fingerprints. Even identical twins, who look exactly the same, have different fingerprints.

Shall we swap?

5

My eyes

The two eyes in your head are the things that you use to see. They send messages to your brain about the world around you. Eyelashes and eyelids are there to protect your eyes.

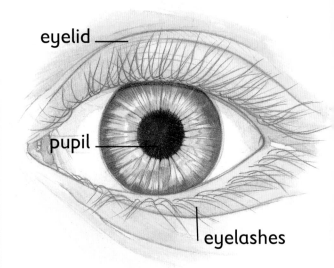

eyelid

pupil

eyelashes

Fabulous Facts

Eye to eye

An eyeball is about the same size and shape as a big grape. The pupil is the part of the eye that lets light in.

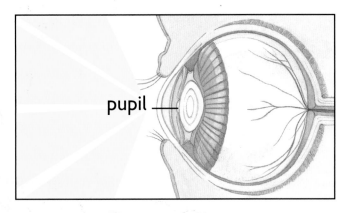

pupil

Wow!

1. Hold out your thumb and look at an object behind it.
2. Close each eye, one at a time.
3. As you close each eye, the object seems to move because you are seeing it from a different angle!

Keep still please!

My ears

The outside parts of your ears collect sounds from the air. Sounds are tiny, invisible waves. These sound waves make the eardrum and small bones inside your ear vibrate, sending the sounds to your brain.

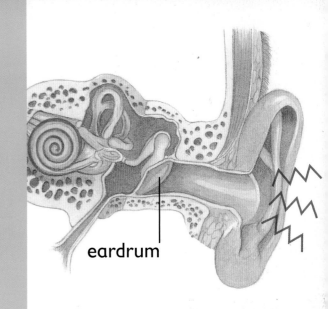

eardrum

Fabulous Facts

Keep it down, please!

People with noisy jobs, like road workers, builders and some musicians, wear ear defenders to protect their ears from very loud sounds!

BANG!

CRASH!

Yuck!

The sticky stuff inside your ear is called earwax. Earwax stops dirt and germs from getting inside the ear.

What can you see?

Lots of earwax!

I can smell and taste

Smell and taste work together. When you eat, tiny parts of your tongue, called taste buds, pick up the flavour of the food. These taste buds and the smells you breathe in through your nose send messages to your brain to tell you what the food tastes like.

Fabulous Facts

Nose trap

Tiny hairs inside your nose trap dust and germs to stop them from getting into your body.

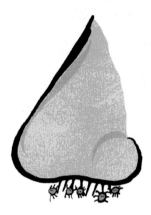

Tongue tinglers

Your tongue can pick up lots of different tastes. The main ones are bitter, salty, sour and sweet.

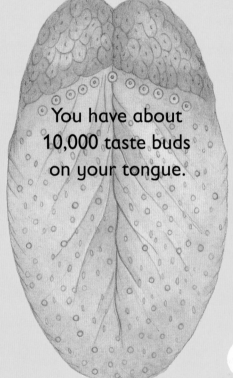

You have about 10,000 taste buds on your tongue.

Hold your nose!

Your sense of smell helps your sense of taste. If you hold your nose while eating something nasty you will hardly be able to taste it!

Yikes!

Sniff, sniff!

Wow!

A dog can smell more than 1,000 times better than a human can. Sniffer dogs are used by the police to help them track down criminals.

9

I can feel with my skin

Your skin covers your whole body. When you touch something, thousands of tiny points under the skin, called nerve endings, tell your brain whether you are touching something hot or cold, hard or soft.

I'm cold!

When you are cold, a tiny muscle pulls your body hairs upright, giving you goosebumps. The hairs then keep warm air next to your skin.

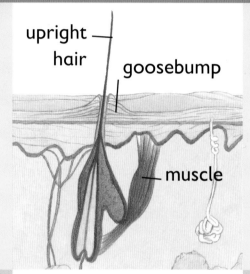

upright hair

goosebump

muscle

Brrrrr!

I'm hot!

When you are hot, the muscle makes your hair lie flat. Sweat glands make sweat. As the sweat dries, it cools your body down.

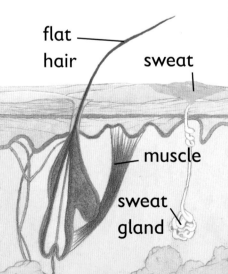

flat hair

sweat

muscle

sweat gland

Phew!

Fabulous Facts

Keep out!

Your skin is a barrier that protects the inside of your body. It also keeps germs out.

I can't get in!

Yuck!

You are losing bits of dead skin all the time. In fact, most of the dust in your house is old flakes of skin! New skin cells are always growing. It takes about a month for all your skin to be replaced.

On your nerves

Your nerves do the important job of telling you when you are hurt. When you feel pain, your body knows it must try to look after the injured area.

Fab scabs

When you cut yourself, your body makes a scab over the cut. Your skin grows back underneath, then the scab falls off.

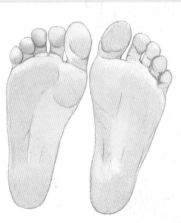

Tough feet

Your skin is thickest on the bottom of your feet. It is thinnest on your eyelids.

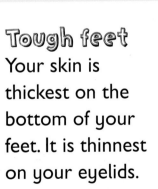

My hair

Your hair grows out of tiny holes in your skin, called follicles. The hair on your head grows about 2 millimetres every week.

hair

follicle

Fabulous Facts

Fancy follicles

Your hair type depends on the shape of the follicles in your skin. If the follicle is round, your hair is straight. A thin, flat follicle makes curly hair.

I wish I had your hair!

I wish I had your hair!

Super styles

Because hair keeps growing, some people like to try lots of different hairstyles!

12

Wow!

A whole head of hair is so strong it can hold about 12 tonnes (roughly the weight of two elephants). So Rapunzel's hair would easily hold her prince!

My nails

Your nails protect the tips of your fingers and toes. Even though they look completely different, your skin, hair and nails are all made of the same thing – keratin.

Fabulous Facts

Fast fingernails

Your fingernails grow 2 to 3 millimetres every month but your toenails only grow about 1 millimetre. Nails grow more quickly in summer than in winter.

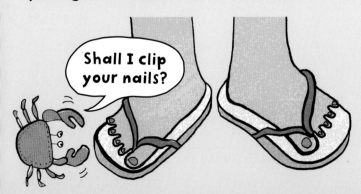

Shall I clip your nails?

Yuck!

The longest nails ever grown were 9.85 metres long when all put together. That's about the same length as a bus!

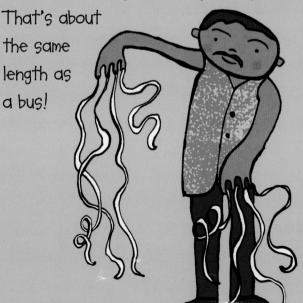

My skeleton

Without bones your body would be all floppy. The bones of your skeleton hold you up, protect your organs and help you to move.

Skull

The area of bone that makes your head. Your skull is made up of 22 separate bones.

Spine

The spine is made up of 33 bones. It is also known as your backbone.

Joints

The part of your body where two bones meet. Joints are like hinges that move with your muscles. There are about 360 joints in your body, including knees and elbows.

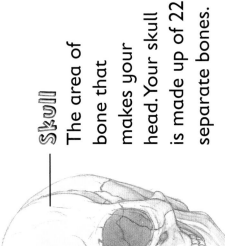

Hand
Each hand has 27 bones.

Broken bones
Your bones are very strong but sometimes they break. Bones heal if they get broken, but bigger bones need to be supported in a plaster cast.

My leg itches!

Foot
You have 26 bones in each foot.

Wow!
You shrink by about 1 centimetre every day! This is because the bones of your spine get squashed together. Don't worry! They stretch out again while you sleep.

15

My heart and lungs

Your heart is a muscle near the middle of your chest. Its job is to pump blood all around your body. Your lungs take in a gas, called oxygen, from the air, and pass it into your blood.

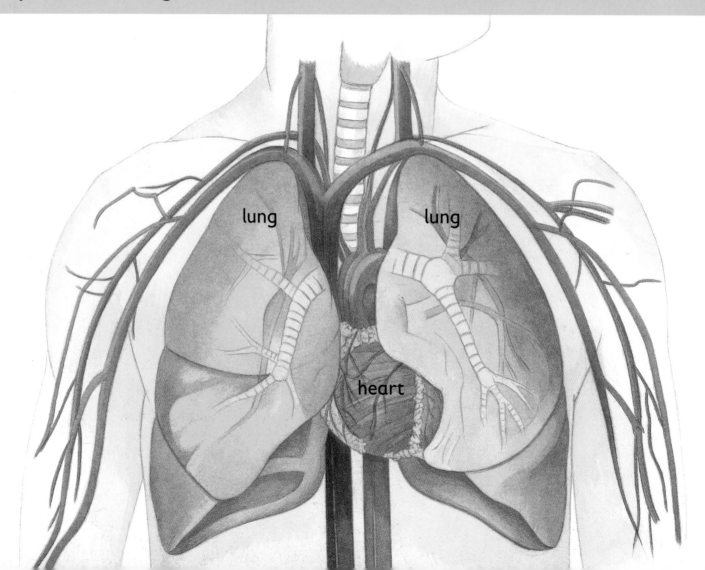

Fabulous Facts

Breathing in

When you breathe in, air goes up your nose, down your windpipe and into your lungs. Your chest gets bigger as your lungs fill with air.

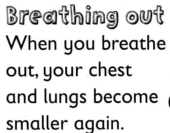

Breathing out

When you breathe out, your chest and lungs become smaller again.

Coughs and sneezes

When you cough or sneeze, your lungs are helping to clear dust and dirt from your airway.

Hand on your heart

Your heart is about the same size as your fist. An adult's heart beats about 70 times a minute.

Wow!

You have about 3 litres of blood in your body. An adult has about 5 litres.

17

My brain

Your brain controls the other parts of your body. It also stores all sorts of information, from your name and age to what you did last week. This is called your memory. Different parts of your brain let you do different things.

hearing

speaking

moving

learning

smelling

touching

seeing

tasting

Fabulous Facts

Soft brain
Your brain is soft and squishy, which is why you have a hard skull to protect it.

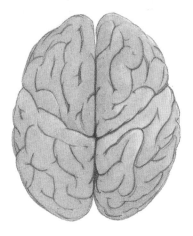

Wow!
Your brain is much faster and more powerful than any computer.

I win!

Left and right
Your brain is made up of two halves joined together. The left half controls the right side of your body and the right half controls the left side.

Sense signals
Your brain organizes the messages from your senses to tell you what you can see, touch and hear.

Nice, soft kitty!

Purr!

I need to eat and drink

The food you eat gives you the energy you need to do all the things you want to do. You need to eat the right foods and drink lots of water.

1 Chewed food goes down a tube to your stomach (tummy).

2 Juices in your stomach mush up your food.

3 The mushy food goes from your stomach into tubes called your intestines.

4 The intestines take out some things that your body needs from the food.

5 The bits of the food that your body does not need come out as poo and wee.

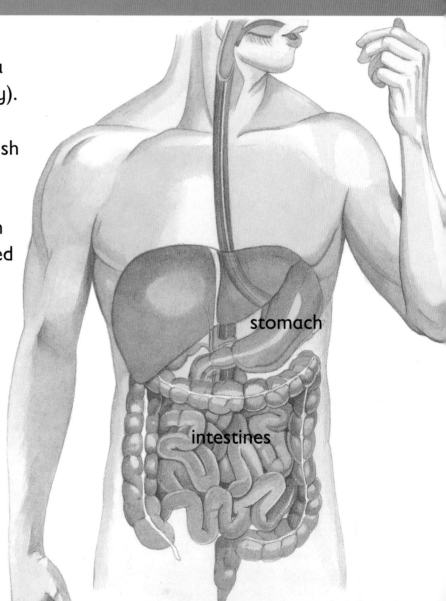

stomach

intestines

Fabulous Facts

Mouth machine

Teeth called incisors and canines cut and tear food up into small pieces. Big teeth called molars chew it up. Saliva makes food easier to swallow and helps your body get the good stuff from your food.

Yum!

Ouch!

Bacteria in your mouth create acid that can harm your teeth. It is important to keep your teeth nice and clean!

Wow!

It takes about a day for a meal to pass through your body!

I'm still here!

Fab foods

Your body needs lots of different foods.

These foods keep you healthy.

These give your body energy.

These make your bones strong.

These help your muscles grow.

21

I can move

Your muscles help your body to move. Your biggest muscles are wrapped around your bones. When your brain tells them to, muscles pull on your bones to make your skeleton move. Taking just one step uses about 200 different muscles in your body!

Fabulous Facts

Mega muscles!

You have about 640 muscles that move when you tell them to. You have hundreds more that move without you thinking — one of them is your heart.

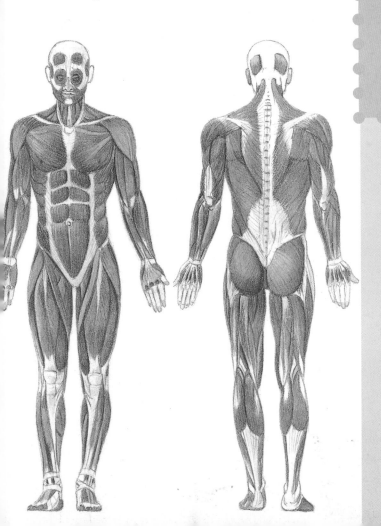

Wow!

Some people have very strong muscles. In strongman contests, competitors pull trucks, and even planes, just using their muscle strength!

Happy face!

A frown uses a lot more muscles in your face than a smile does. So keep smiling!

Cheer up!

23

I am growing

You are growing all the time and you will not stop growing until you are an adult. People grow at different speeds. Your body changes most when you are a child.

At two years old, you are about half the height you will be when you're a grown up.

Teenagers grow up to 9 centimetres a year. Growth stops between the ages of sixteen and twenty-one.

Each generation of adults is almost 2 centimetres taller than the one before.

Fabulous Facts

Milk teeth

Children have about 25 milk teeth. As you grow up these fall out and are replaced with adult teeth. Adults have up to 32 teeth.

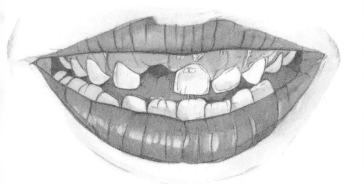

Miracle of life

Babies grow inside their mothers for nine months before they are born.

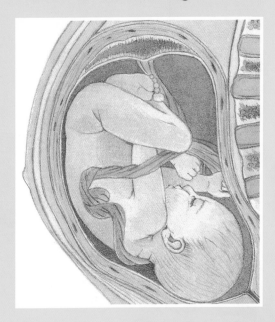

Shrinking

Older people can actually get shorter. This happens when the space between the bones in their spine gets a bit smaller.

Hello dear!

Wow!

More babies than ever are being born every day and lots of people are living longer, too!

Ahhh!

I need sleep

You need sleep to stay healthy. While you are asleep, your body is resting, growing and repairing. It is also getting ready for another busy day, and your brain is sorting out your thoughts.

Sweet dreams
Everyone has a few dreams each night but we don't always remember them.

26

Fabulous Facts

Yawning

You yawn when you are tired or bored. Nobody really knows why, but it is catching!

Night walks

Some people walk in their sleep. It usually only lasts a few moments, and they often wake up safely back in their beds!

Zzzzzz

Snoring happens when your throat is partly blocked by your tongue. Your tongue and throat muscles rattle as the air passes by.

Sssh! You're keeping me awake!

Wow!

You will spend about 22 years of your life asleep!

Sleep tight

Babies and children need about 11 hours sleep each night to stay healthy. An adult needs about eight hours sleep.

Record breakers

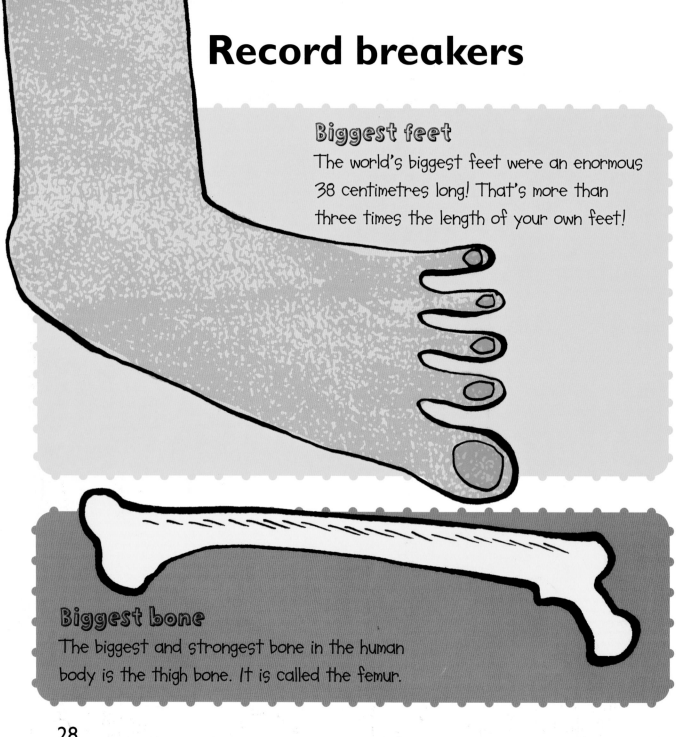

Biggest feet
The world's biggest feet were an enormous 38 centimetres long! That's more than three times the length of your own feet!

Biggest bone
The biggest and strongest bone in the human body is the thigh bone. It is called the femur.

Biggest muscle

Your biggest muscle is in your bottom! It is called your gluteus maximus.

Longest hair

The longest strand of hair ever recorded was 5.63 metres long – about the length of a minibus!

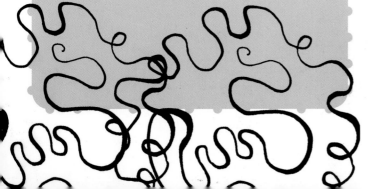

Tallest man

The world's tallest man is 251 centimetres tall. The average man is about 177 centimetres tall!

Funny bodies!

What instrument do skeletons play?

The trom-bone!

What kind of hair do oceans have?

Wavy!

What did one eye say to the other?

Something between us smells!

What has a bottom at the top?

Your legs!

How do you get a baby astronaut to fall asleep?

Rock it!

Why was the nose tired?

Because it kept running!

Glossary

acid   A liquid that dissolves substances. The acids in your stomach dissolve food so your body can use it.

airway   The part of the body between your mouth, nose and lungs.

bacteria   Tiny living things that can be found in and on the body. Some bacteria can cause your body harm.

energy   The power that the body needs to work.

germs   Tiny living things that can cause your body harm.

keratin   Fibre-like substance that makes up skin, hair and nails.

nerve   Part of the network that carries messages around your body, to and from your brain.

organ   A part of the body that has a special job to do. Your brain is an organ, as are your lungs.

saliva   A liquid made in the mouth that helps you to eat food.

senses   What the body uses to understand the world. The senses are sight, smell, hearing, taste and touch.

vibrate   To move very quickly to and fro.

Index